T0208770

GOD'S MOST BEAUTIFUL CREATURE: WOMAN

DR. GILBERT H. EDWARDS, SR.

authorHOUSE®

AuthorHouse™
1663 Liberty Drive
Bloomington, IN 47403
www.authorhouse.com
Phone: 1 (800) 839-8640

Published by AuthorHouse   06/15/2020

ISBN: 978-1-7283-6501-5 (sc)
ISBN: 978-1-7283-6502-2 (e)

Print information available on the last page.

Scripture quotations marked KJV are from the Holy Bible, King James Version (Authorized Version). First published in 1611. Quoted from the KJV Classic Reference Bible, Copyright © 1983 by The Zondervan Corporation.

This book is printed on acid-free paper.

DEDICATION

This book is dedicated to all who read this book.

CONTENTS

PREFACE

For some time now, I have been studying women. How they are good for men and also could be dangerous to men. Men have been made happy by them and with them. I have also seen men fall or feel less about themselves because of women. My study goes back to the beginning of time in the Garden of Eden.

God placed the newly created man in a garden especially created and designed as a comfortable home for him. God created woman to be his companion, to share life with him in a complementary, mutually fulfilling relationship. God desired for them a rich and full life. God expected them to live in the ways of righteousness that He set forth. But the fateful choice of the woman caused her and her husband to fall from the Grace of God. This is the reason I'm writing this study on the behavior of women.

Introduction

The focus here is on the consequences of associating with an immoral woman. Eventually, moral corruption robs us of the ability to distinguish right from wrong. A man that findeth a wife, findest a good thing. But, sometimes you can find trouble, that's if she is not the right mate. Among such tragedies is the disaster of sexual sins with immoral women and wayward wives. Such sin begins with flirtatious looks and ends with disastrous punishment. They set traps for men. Solomon tells us in the Song of Songs about the love and beauty of the woman, and the beauty of her body parts.

It also gives new definition to love. Love and sexual union are a God-given privilege for a man and a woman to share. God made man and woman physically attractive to each other. The characteristics should be noticed of a wise woman and a foolish woman. The wise woman builds her house, but a foolish woman tears her house down. A man must study a woman to know how she thinks and what she wants. The accomplishments of a wise and industrious woman are magnificent to behold and is a source of strength and encouragement to all who know her. A wise woman's potential reaches out to, too many fields of endeavor, but all women are not like that. There are some strange women out there in the woods (world).

A man must know his wife in order to deal with her. It must be according to the knowledge of the nature and duties of the marriage relationship. You will have to know a lion before you can tame it. Not saying that women are lions, but they are creatures. This is why it is necessary to bring that out in this study.

The main part of this study is about a young black boy who runs off into the woods (the world) among these beautiful creatures.

CHAPTER I

THE ORIGIN OF WOMAN

It is stated in the Bible:

> "And the LORD God said, "It is not good that the man should be alone; I will make him a help meet for him." And out of the ground the LORD God formed every beast of the field and every fowl of the air; and brought them unto Adam to see what he would call them: and whatsoever Adam called every living creature that was the name thereof. And Adam gave names to all cattle, and to the fowl of the air and to every beast of the field; but for Adam there was not found a help meet for him. And the LORD God caused a deep sleep to fall upon Adam, and he slept: and he took one of his ribs, and closed up the flesh instead thereof; and the rib, which the LORD God had taken from man, made he a woman, and brought her unto the man." (Genesis 2:18-22 KJV)

It is not good that the man should be alone; from this verse it is deduce that marriage is a divine institution, a holy estate in which alone man lives his true and complete life.

<u>A help meet for him</u>: God did not make woman to be man's shadow or subordinate, but his other self; his helper in a sense which no other creature on earth can be.

<u>Meet for him</u>: To match him; or fit to associate with him. Man needed companionship.

Woman was not formed from the dust of the earth, but from man's body. We have here a wonderfully conceived allegory designed to set for the moral and social relation of the sexes to each other. The dependence of woman upon man, her close relationship to him and the foundation existing in nature for the attachment springing up between them, the woman is formed out of the man's side. It is the wife's natural duty to be a help to her husband, and it is the husband's natural duty to ever cherish and defend his wife, as part of his own self.

> "And the rib, which the Lord God had taken from the man, made he a woman, and brought her unto the man (Genesis 2:22 KJV)."

<u>Made</u>: built; this teaches that God has endowed woman with greater intuition than He has man. Man was created from the dust of the earth. But the thing that eternally matters is the breath of divine and everlasting life that He (God) breathed into the being coming from the dust. By virtue of that divine impact, a new and distinctive creature made its

appearance – man, dowered with an immortal soul. The sublime revelation of the unique worth and dignity of man, contained in <u>Genesis 1:27 (KJV)</u>, (So God created man in His own image, in the image of God created He him.)

The making of woman:

> "So God created man (human being) in his own image, in the image of God created he him; male and female created he them." (Genesis 1:27 KJV)

God created He him, (single) male and female created He them (plural). So in <u>him</u>, was <u>them</u>. Adam (human being) had both male and female traits in him. When the woman was made from out of the man, it seems that God took out of man the feminine traits and made woman. Woman was made to be the help-mate of man. A wife is a man's other self and all that man's nature demands for its completions physically, socially and spiritually. She is womanly in character and femininity, as applied to man, one who is effeminate, timid or weak; a female attendant. The whole body of a woman is beautiful; her eyes, whether they are blue, green, gray, brown or black, and her hair around her face to match her complexion, blond, black, brown or red hair.

As the man is from the dust of the ground, the woman is indirectly from the ground, because she was taken from the man. Just as the man, the woman also as the man consists of body and soul in one complete person (Genesis 2:7 KJV). The body of the man is of the dust of the ground and the woman also, but indirectly (Genesis 3:19 KJV). She has eyes that see, ears that hear and a heart that beats and sends blood through the blood stream to the lungs to be purified and throughout the entire body to build up its tissues. The heart is a delicate nervous system that carries messages to and from the brain, and all members so constructed as to serve their purpose most admirably (Psalm 139:14 KJV).

In the beginning, God made a man and a woman, and joined them in wedlock to be one flesh, (Genesis 2:18, 21-34 KJV) that they should be fruitful and multiply and replenish the earth (Genesis 1:27, 28 KJV). Since then, men and woman are no longer created in the same manner as Adam and Eve were created, but they are begotten and born of their parents; Adam begat a son (Genesis 5:3 KJV), and Eve bore Cain (Genesis 4:1 KJV). Parents beget not only the body, but living children; therefore, the national soul is passed on by parents to their children. Nevertheless, it is God who forms the child in the mother's womb (Jeremiah 1:5 KJV), and gives it life and breath (Acts 17:25 KJV; Zechariah 12:1 KJV).

In his original state man was very good in every respect, so was the woman. The physical condition of his body was perfect, so was the woman; there was no weak and defective organ, no germ of disease or death. Except Christ, Adam and Eve, before the fall, were the only human beings that ever were perfectly healthy in their bodies and perfectly sane in their minds.

Both man and woman were created in the image of God (Genesis 1:27 KJV), which being a spiritual likeness, had its seat in the soul, and was reflected in their lives. It consisted of blissful knowledge of God (Colossians 3:10 KJV), and in perfect righteousness and true holiness of life (Ephesians 4:24 KJV). There was no evil, no sin in man nor woman; they were innocent; not ashamed of their nakedness (Genesis 2:25 KJV). Man knew the will of God and was fully able to conform to it in thought, word and deed.

The mutual relationship between the man and the woman was ideal. Each of them fully understanding and observing the duties and restrictions of his and her position, and regarding each other as a precious gift of their creator.

> "And the Lord God said, It is not good that the man should be alone; I will make him an help meet for him." (Genesis 2:18 KJV)

Man is the image and glory of God; but the woman is the glory of man. For the man is not of the woman; but the woman is of the man. Neither was the man created for the woman; but the woman for the man (I Corinthians 11:7-9 KJV). From this it appears that also in the state of integrity, the man was the head of the wife and she was a help meet for him. The full measure of happiness, which the estate of matrimony was intended to bring to both, was realized while Adam and Eve remained sinless.

The woman was born in a beautiful place, "The Garden of Eden." This garden is known as "Paradise"; an enclosure or park eastward; the home of the earliest civilization; or situated east of Eden; Eden meaning "delight." What I'm trying to say is, this beautiful creature (woman) was put in a beautiful place. She was beautiful and now surrounded by beautiful things. The phrase "Garden of Eden" became in the course of time descriptive of any place possessing beauty and fertility. In later Jewish literature, it signifies the heavenly paradise where the souls of the righteous repose in felicity.

Chapter II

The Description of these Creatures

The woman was made from a portion of the man's side; therefore, it seems that she shares the same physical nature but with some differences. She is that feminine part that was taken out of man. She is being referred as physically weaker than man (I Peter 3:7 KJV). She has a mild and beautiful face, a tender voice, and a soft body. Her intelligence is modest, refined, pacific, yielding, gentle and tender.

In the Book of the Song of Solomon, he points out and describes the very parts of her body:

(1) The cheeks – cheeks are adorned with circlets; a circular band made of precious metal, or her cheeks are beautiful with earrings. Her neck with strings of jewels. Her neck is like a land mark; the husband recalls his wife's upright posture and how it enhances her natural beauty. He likened her to the Tower of David, a mighty and tall fortress that

served as a guiding land mark for travelers (Song of Solomon 4:4 KJV).

(2) Eyes – some eyes are blue, black, grey, brown and hazel.

(3) Hair – black, red-headed, blond, brunette and brown; long and flowing, like the hair of goats as they descend the slopes up a mountain (Song of Songs 4:1 KJV).

(4) Lips – her lips drip sweetness; honey and milk are under her tongue; alluding to the deepest mysteries of the law and teaching.

(5) Teeth – Her teeth are like a select flock which has come up from the washing; they are all perfect, and not a single one is blemished.

(6) Breasts – Spiritual nourishment as a mother's breasts nourish her infant; alluding to the two tablets of the Law. Every part of her body is lovely. Her feet are lovely in sandals where you can see them. Her thighs are rounder, they are like jewels, and it seems as the handiwork of a craftsman. Her navel is a round goblet which never lacks blended wine. Her belly is like a heap of wheat hedged in with roses. Her two breasts are like twin deer. Her neck is like an ivory tower, her eyes like the pools in Cheshbon by the Beth-Rabim Gate, which quenches the people's spiritual thirst in much the same manner as the abundant watering troughs of Cheshbon

Bath-Rabim Gate quench the many flocks which pasture in that region.

She is attractive as King Solomon states in Song of Solomon 1:5 (KJV). Just as rose petals are beautiful despite being pierced by the thorns of adjacent stems, so too, she can remain steadfast in her faith despite the negative spiritual influence of the idolatrous society in which they live. She can remain faithful despite the many hardships she endures.

Chapter III

The Purpose of the Woman

"It is not good for man to be alone." From this verse, Genesis 2:18 (KJV), it states that marriage is a divine institution, a holy estate, in which man alone lives his true and complete life. So, the woman is for the healing of man's loneliness and also to make him complete. Man needed someone who could associate with him or correspond to him. We have here a wonderfully conceived allegory designed to set forth the moral and social relation of the sexes to each other, the dependence of woman upon man, her close relationship to him and the foundation existing in nature for the attachment springing up between them. Because the woman was taken out of man's side, it is the wife's natural duty to be a hand, ready at all times to be a "help" to her husband.

The woman was made to be man's glory (I Corinthians 11:7 KJV). Her excellence is an expression of his dignity and worth, since she was formed of him and for him. Verse 10 KJV, "For this cause ought the woman to have power on her head because of the angels." Power that is, a veil as the token of her husband's rightful authority over her and of her subjection to him.

Paul states:

> "Likewise, ye wives, be in subjection to your own husbands: that if any obey not the word, they also may without the word be won by the conversation of the wives." (I Peter 3:1 KJV)

Be in subjection to your own husbands; treat them as the rightful head of the family.

The word: the scriptures and the preaching of the Gospel.

Be won: led to embrace the Gospel. The woman's conversation should be chaste, pure deportment, fearful, a reverential demeanor such as becomes the wife; your husband needs that.

The woman is to adorn herself for her husband; instead of outward adornments visible to man, let it consist in the inward spiritual state of the heart, invisible to sense, which alone God regards. (I Peter 3:3-4 KJV)(I Samuel 16:7 KJV)

Sarah obeyed Abraham her husband, calling him Lord; therefore, acknowledging her subjection to him as her rightful head. (Genesis 18:12; I Corinthians 11:3 KJV). The most excellent, lovely and enduring ornaments of women are not those which are external, but those which are internal- purity of heart, meekness, contentment and delight in doing good. The woman is to help her husband to replenish the earth, that is to bear children and to teach good things; that they teach the young woman to be sober, to love their husband, to love their children, to be discreet, chaste keepers at home, good, obedient to their own husband that the word of God be not blasphemed (Titus 2:3-6 KJV).

Elderly women should be able to give counseling to girls and young married women. The woman is to make man better. God gave the woman great wisdom to help her husband (Proverbs 14:1; 31:10-27 KJV). A woman of valor, divine presence, or to gather knowledge for the soul, her husband's heart relies on her and he has no lack of gain. She is not vindictive, repaying him a good turn in kind, but not reciprocating when he acts unkindly towards her. She is good to him, never bad. She helps her husband bear the burden of supporting a household by selling her handiwork in distant markets where greater profits may be earned. She works from home, which her husband has provided for her. She does not neglect her domestic responsibilities, but rises before dawn and nurtures her household. She sets her mind on a goal and does not deviate from it until she has achieved it. As a direct consequence of her unwavering support for her husband's teaching study of the Gospel, he becomes one of the most prominent scholars in the land; or the graceful clothing she makes for him causes him to stand out among his fellow scholars. I told you she can make you better. Her purpose was to make her husband be the best that he can be. This woman deserves to be blessed.

Chapter IV

The Characteristics of the Woman

The first woman Eve, seemed to show the power of women to lead weak men. After she had partaken of the forbidden fruit, she also gave it to Adam and he too ate it, therefore, sharing in her guilt. In this act, we have an excellent example of woman's impulsiveness and man's inclination to follow the woman wherever she leads, even into sin. After Eve did wrong, she displayed the natural tendency of a woman, blamed not herself for her wrong doings, but those around her. Still she was able to rise to the dream of her destiny as a wife and mother.

Remember, the significant fact is that this woman was set in a pattern of sublime religious truths. She was made for man to fill his loneliness. God was obligated to make for man a helper who was his equal and who shared in the same processes of creation in which she shared. She was able to have a close relationship with man because she was taken from the place nearest to his heart. Therefore, her character is to be in oneness with her husband. Eve arises from the rib of Adam, beautiful of form and figure and with Paradise as her birthplace. All of the great epochs in a woman's life, her marriage, mating, and motherhood unfolds in all of their completeness in the Genesis account of Eve (the first woman). In Eve all the elemental questions of life, birth and death, even sin and temptation, are sown in their human dimension.

According to Eve, women are easy to yield to temptations. When the serpent tempted Eve, she followed the path to evil. Instead of staying with God who watched over her truest interests, she turned to a serpent. But, later in life she turned back to God. Eve experienced pain in the child birth of her first son, Cain and then Abel. When her first son, Cain killed his brother Abel, she experienced anxieties and heartaches, but Eve knew that God still existed. She waited for God to fulfill His plan in her life. She then gave birth to Seth, his name meaning "to appoint" or "to establish", and she took new courage in the fact. For she said, "God hath appointed me another seed instead of Abel, whom Cain slew." A great seed this was to be traced back to the line Seth. She lived on in Seth, the strongest of her children, and in the great line of Seth's descendants, who called "upon the name of the Lord."

Sarah, the Mother of Nations – her character distinctly portrayed in history of man's spiritual development is Sarah, the beloved wife of Abraham. Sarah's life was one continuous trial of her faith in God's promise that she was to be the Mother of Nations.

The woman loves good things (Genesis 3:6 KJV), and a woman can be good, but there is a good inclination and an evil inclination. As I said, the woman loves good things. If she sees it and desires it, she will go for it (Genesis 3:6 KJV). The woman saw – the serpent did not tell her to eat the fruit. The woman looked (with her beautiful eyes) upon the tree with a new longing. It was good to eat, a delight to the eyes and it would give wisdom.

The Evil Inclinations of the Woman

(1) A Strange Woman (Proverbs 2:16 KJV)

> She speaks with seductive words. She has left the partner of her youth and has ignored the covenant she made before God. Her house leads down to death and her paths to the spirits of the dead. She is just strange, so in a woman's character, she can act strange.

(2) An Evil Woman (Proverbs 6:24 KJV)

> It is in her character to trap men with her eyes, so don't let her take you with her eyes. She can be immoral in nature. Such sin begins with flirtations, looks and ends with disastrous punishment.

(3) A Whorish Woman (Proverbs 6:26 KJV)

> She is capable of whorishness, which is the characteristic of a prostitute.

(4) A Foolish Woman (Proverbs 9:13 KJV)

She is clamorous, simple and knows nothing. She sits where she can be seen; calling out to those who pass by. She looks for someone who is as simple as she is, and that lacks judgment. This woman has the characteristic of a take –over spirit and will take the man's authority (I Timothy 2:12 KJV). I do know that this took place in Paul's day, but verse 13 said that Adam was first formed; an indication that he is the head of woman, and that the office of teaching and governing belongs to him (I Corinthians 11:8-9 KJV). She was deceived by the serpent in the first transgression. The serpent first assailed the woman as being most open to his arts, and having deceived her, he made use of her to persuade her husband. She is easy to be persuaded (Genesis 3:13, 17 KJV). Then Paul in verse 15 states; she shall be saved in childbearing. Paul says this with reference to the original curse pronounced upon the woman; ". . . In sorrow shalt thou bring forth children. . . "(Genesis 3:16 KJV). So in verse 12, Paul is saying not me, but Paul, that it is the revealed will of God that public religious teachers should be men not women. He has allotted to them different spheres of action, and the perfection of each consists not in aspiring or submitting to occupy the place of the other, but in performing their own appropriate duties. The author is stating what Paul is teaching in his day. But it is the spirit of the woman to take over, if she can find weakness in the man.

Let's start with Jezebel. When she found that her husband Ahab seemed to be too weak, as the King of Israel, and looking sad and rejected, in so many words she said slide over, let me show you how to do it. In I Kings 21:5 (KJV), his wife Jezebel came to him and asked him, "What has saddened you that you refuse to eat?" In verse 6 he answered; "When I spoke to Naboth, the Jezreelite", Ahab told her, "I said to him, sell me your vineyard for money, or if you prefer, I'll give you another vineyard for it." (I see him as a little boy pouting to his mother.) But he said to me, "I will not give you my vineyard." Ahab made Naboth sound more unyielding than he really was by omitting his reason (God forbid that I should give away my family's hereditary estate to you.) In verse 7, his wife Jezebel takes over. "Now is the time for you to rule over Israel", his wife Jezebel told (with authority) to him. "Get up, eat something, and you'll feel better. I'll get you the vineyard of Naboth the Jezreelite." She did it, took over and got Ahab in trouble just as Eve did to Adam in the Garden of Eden.

(5) A Brawling Woman (Proverbs 19:14 KJV)

It is better to live on a corner of the roof than share a house with a quarrelsome wife. It is in her character.

(6) A Contentious and Angry Woman (Proverbs 21:19 KJV)

> It's better to live in the desert. If you can't keep her happy, this characteristic will spring out of her because it is there.

The Evil Character of Woman

Lot's Wife

Lot's wife was a woman who ate and drank and lived for things of the world. Her husband was a rich and influential man (Genesis 13:10-11 KJV); because of this, we can see Lot's wife as a worldly, selfish woman in her behavior. One who spent lavishly and entertained elaborately. She looked back and lingered behind to be overtaken by brimstone and fire. She could not be influenced by the warning of the angels or by the pleadings of her husband. She is noticed as the woman who looked back and refuses to move forward; the woman who faced toward salvation, yet, still turns to look longingly on material things that she has left behind.

Potiphar's Wife

A woman remembered only by her wickedness. When she attempted infidelity (in her behavior) with young Joseph during her husband's absence from home, she disgraced the distinction she might have borne, that of respected wife of the Chief of the Egyptian King's bodyguard. She may be as worldly as Lot's wife or worse. Because of her husband's riches, she became a spoiled, selfish woman. Potiphar's wife had no appreciation of good character. After her husband had departed, she sought to become familiar with young Joseph. And one day, when no one was around the house, she said to Joseph, "Lie with me." (Genesis 39:7 KJV) Potiphar's wife was wicked in character. When Joseph resisted her, she was angered. Day-by-day she invited him into her private room; but, he always resisted her advances because he knew God had great purposes for him. She was very wicked and when she could not entice Joseph, she caught his garment in her hand and held it; but he fled leaving it with her. Potiphar's wife who had not received what she asked for determined to hurt Joseph. She screamed loudly so others could hear her in the household saying, "See, he hath brought in a Hebrew unto us to mock us; he came in unto me to lie with me, and I cried with a loud voice." (Genesis 39:14 KJV). Potiphar's wife kept Joseph's garment and showed it to her husband. When Potiphar saw it he cast Joseph into prison, because his wife had lied on Joseph. (Genesis 39:17-18 KJV). These are the last words of this despicable woman, who has become a symbol of the faithless wife. Her obscurity, except for her wickedness is final. Her own silence, in face of young Joseph's term in prison, is even greater admission to the bad character of Potiphar's wife, who was not only a sensualist but also a coward who could not admit her own guilt.

Zipporah – Moses' Wife

She is believed to be a woman of violent temper who had little sympathy with the religious convictions of her distinguished husband because of the words she spoke:

> "Then Zipporah took a flint and cut off the
> foreskin of her son, and cast it at his feet; and
> she said: surely a bridegroom of blood art thou
> to me; so he let him alone. Then she said; a
> husband of blood in regard of the circumcision
> (Exodus 4:25-26 KJV).

Moses fell suddenly into a serious illness. Many commentators connect this sudden illness of Moses with postponing, for some reason, the circumcision of his son. Moses being disabled by illness; Zipporah his wife, performed the ceremony. We believe that Moses was very ill and his life was in danger because he was troubled because of his wife. A Midianite has refused to allow the circumcision of their sons, a symbol of the covenant between God and His people. And Moses, now called by God to the leadership of His people, was troubled because he had neglected the sacred duty of circumcision which was not practiced by his wife's people. She came from a Midian background (Exodus 2:16 KJV). Maybe the delay in circumcision was due to Zipporah's prejudices. When she saw her husband so very ill, she doubtlessly believed that God was angered with him because he had not circumcised himself; that is when she took a piece of flint and circumcised her son herself. So I believe that she was wicked and prejudice in character.

Miriam – Moses' Sister

In the beginning of her life, she was of good character. I believe some period of time after the passing across the Red Sea, her character had changed completely. She has had a spiritual fall. She has spoken against her brother Moses.

The limitations in Miriam's character came into clear focus in this period of her life. Now she is no more a leader in triumphant, but now a leader in jealousy and bitterness. She is believed to be jealous and bitter of her brother's position with God. With Aaron, her brother, she murmured:

> ". . . Hath the Lord indeed spoken only by Moses? hath He not spoken also by us? And the Lord heard it." Numbers 12:2 KJV)

In this delineation of the envious, bitter side of Miriam's character, following so soon after the courageous now comes this period of the woman who had sung to God so joyfully. This shows the perfect example of the woman's mixed nature of good and evil. For Miriam, the foul vice of envy had spread over her whole character. Bad character can lead to bad things. (Numbers 12:10 KJV)

Jezebel, Ahab's Wife

Jezebel brought with her into Israel customs of fearful cruelty and revolt. In her evil power over her husband, King Ahab, it showed that she was a domineering person. She became the master of her husband and in turn the despot of the nation. (I Kings 18:4,13 KJV) Jezebel was so infuriated when her priests were defeated that she threatened Elijah's life. He fled from her wrath to the wilderness. She had a dominating spirit in her character. She continued to dominate Israel from her ivory-decorated palace. Jezebel had plotted treacherously to gain her way (I Kings 21:15 KJV); but because of her evil ways, she was faced with the most gruesome death of all. (II Kings 9:31 KJV)

Athaliah

Athaliah, another woman who was extreme in wickedness, seemed that evil ran in her veins. She was the daughter of King Ahab and Jezebel. Athaliah grew up in an atmosphere that completely denied the one true God. She was introduced to Baal worship by her mother. She promoted her Baal worship among her people. Athaliah was a wicked counselor to her son (II Chronicles 23:3 KJV). When her son died, Athaliah seized the throne and resolved to destroy "all the seed royal." His own blood relations among whom were her own grandchildren. Athaliah also had a terrible death just as her mother Jezebel. She was slain as she was entering the horses' gate by the palace, close by the temple. The horses trampled over her body where she lay dead at the gates. Athaliah bore a singular resemblance to her mother Jezebel, who was abandoned to the dogs. Athaliah was left in a horse path, to be trampled upon. Athaliah is recorded as that wicked woman (II Chronicles 24:7 KJV).

Herodias

Herodias, the wife of Philip; her character was of an evil influence of a heartless, determined woman in a high position. As the second wife of Herod Antipas, she demands through her daughter the head of John the Baptist, because he had denied her marriage. She receives this ghastly gift on a platter. Herodias was descended from a line of wicked people. Her first marriage, according to history, had been to her half-uncle Herod Philip. She entered into a second incestuous and illicit union when she divorced him to marry his half-brother Herod Antipas who was the step-brother of her father, Aristobulus. To Herodia's first union had been born her dancing daughter, to whom Josephus gives the name of Salome. She must have been brought up in the evil atmosphere of the family. We are told that she excelled in sensuous dancing.

History shows us that evil ran all through Herodias' life. She was a granddaughter of Herod the Great, who carved out his empire with a sword and sought to destroy the child Jesus (Matthew 2:13 KJV). Herodias was willing to pay any price for a regal position regardless of the principles or people involved. She persuaded Herod Antipas to divorce his wife and she in turn divorced her husband and left Rome for Tiberias, the Capital city of the province of Galilee, where Herod Antipas was now Tetrarch. It was said that great artists have depicted Herodias as a beautiful woman, who wore a crown from which a thin veil fell in long graceful folds. Beneath it was her dark hair adorned with pearls. Her dress was of a flowing rich regal fabric. Herodias could not forget John the Baptist's rebuke of her marriage. Vindictive as well as cruel, she determined that she would get rid of this man; and so she entered upon her foul scheme. Her daughter danced for Herod in the palace on his birthday, as Herodias sat looking on. The daughter pleased Herod so much that he said to her, ". . . Ask of me whatsoever thou wilt, and I will give it thee." (Mark 6:22 KJV) The daughter asked her mother, "What shall I ask?" And the mother made her ghastly request for "the head of John the Baptist." Herodias had her way. She was the evil influence for both her daughter and her husband and the sole instigator of one of the most horrible crimes ever committed against a just and Holy man. Herodias ended her life in exile and disgrace with her husband. They had lost everything. Her life had followed in evil patterns to the end.

Sapphira

Sapphira's downfall was her love of money. This woman and her husband withheld money for themselves that has been dedicated to the common good. They had agreed with others to share all that they had with one another and to contribute to a common treasury to meet the common needs. (Acts 2:44-45; 4:32 KJV) They were not forced into this agreement, but they had agreed to it voluntarily, and the agreement had become a sacred pledge. Sapphira could not stand a stern test with money. The scripture states:

> "For the love of money is the root of all evil;
> which while some coveted after, they have erred
> from the faith, and pierced themselves through
> with many sorrows." (I Timothy 6:10 KJV)

They did not give it all. They coveted some of the money for themselves and resorted to dishonesty and untruthfulness to keep it. (Acts 5:1, 2 KJV) Sapphira, Ananias' wife, we might make a stronger indictment of her and say that she may have been guiltier than her husband, for it could have been she who chiefly coveted the money. A wife can at times influence her husband; for it is stated, "with his wife's knowledge." Her husband committed evil entirely with her knowledge, and it would also seem with her support, if not at her instigation. In Hebrew, the name Sapphira means "beautiful." Does this give us a sense to what her character might have been?

Ralph Waldo, a practical poet (a beautiful woman), states:

> "Taming her savage mate, planting tenderness,
> hope and eloquence in whom she approaches."

But Sapphira did not live up to her name. When Peter asked Sapphira if the land had been sold for the amount specified by her husband, she answered, "Yes, for so much." (Acts 5:8 KJV) In this dishonest answer she revealed herself as a wife who thought it better to conceal her own and her husband's dishonesty than to be honest with the Church and loyal to God. She pretended to be something she was not.

In the eyes of the people, she appeared generous; but in the eyes of God, she was a hypocrite. It is important that we understand what an extremely important obligation rested upon Sapphira as a leading member of this first Christian church. The sudden death of Sapphira and her husband made others in the Church see what could happen when a husband and a wife become partners in evil and not in truth. They saw what a sin two had arranged was worse than one done singularly.

Drusilla and Bernice

These two evil sisters helped to condemn Paul. When Paul was brought as a prisoner into the judgment hall at Caesarea and accused unjustly of sedition and profanations of the temple, important auditors were two shameless sisters,

Drusilla and Bernice. They were daughters of Herod Agrippa I, the first royal prosecutor of the Church. They were the granddaughters of Herod the Great, who at the time of his birth had sought to destroy the child Jesus. Bernice and her sister Drusilla were nieces of Herod Antipas, who had John the Baptist beheaded at the request of his wife Herodias and her daughter by another marriage.

Drusilla left her husband to marry Felix, a Gentile, and had come to Caesarea to live with him. She, being a Jewish girl. Paul was already there in prison and she wanted to see Paul. Her husband Felix sent for Paul to please his beautiful young wife Drusilla. When Paul came before Felix the second time, his wife Drusilla was with her husband and heard Paul's message concerning the faith in Jesus Christ (Acts 24:24 KJV).

Tradition has it that some years later, Drusilla perished with her son by Felix beneath the Lava in the great eruption of Vesuvius when Pompeii was destroyed. Like her sister, Bernice would be curious to see Paul. (Acts 25:19 KJV) She was a clever woman. She probably was smiling deviously as Festus declared to her brother that all the multitude had cried that Paul "ought not to live any longer." (Acts 25:24 KJV) She was with Agrippa throughout the whole story, spoken by Paul. (Acts 26:18 KJV)

She was there when her brother Agrippa replied, "almost thou persuades me to be a Christian. (Acts 26:28 KJV) She had heard Festus declare that because he had not certain thing to accuse Paul of, he had brought him before King Agrippa. Hearing the gospel that Paul preached gave her an opportunity to change her file. She could have engaged into a spiritual realm with this steadfast Christian Paul, but her conception of what it was to be a Christian was too faint and dim. It did not better her way of life. She continued the same scandalous relationship with her brother. In the Spring of A.D. 66, history further tells us that Bernice was in Jerusalem. It was during the Jewish war, and she performed the one redeeming act in her infamous career. She and other leading Jews went before Cestius to complain of the iniquities of the brutal Florus. She has been depicted as going before him barefooted and with her hair disheveled. But Florus, we are told, paid no attention to the once proud Bernice, and even in her presence, he scourged and murdered Jews. Bernice was reaping what she had sown when she had sat watching others unjustly accuse Paul. Like her sister, she then disappeared into the obscure pages of history, as one of the most shameless women of her time. Bernice and her sister Drusilla never experienced anything but worldly pleasures. In which they paid a heavy price. They came into bible history for one reason, because they were present and occupied influential positions at the trials of the courageous and earnest Christian Paul. Though Paul introduced Bernice and Drusilla to the regenerating power of Jesus Christ, they quickly retreated into the darkness of their own sensual and selfish lives.

The Good Inclinations of the Woman

(1) A Virtuous Woman (Proverbs 31:10 KJV)

> She is a woman of noble character. The accomplishments of a wise and industrious

woman are magnificent to behold, and a source of strength and encouragement to all who know her. It is in her character to work at home, and in her home. In her wisdom she uses her husband's estate to produce a profit. She is not lazy. She is seated by her husband and seeks to help at all times.

(2) A Wise Woman (Proverbs 14:1 KJV)

She works hard, makes difficult decisions, earns and invests money well, is compassionate and helpful to the needy, and has the wisdom to teach other people. It is in her character to earn a high reputation in her family. She is a God fearing woman. She is subject to her husband in all things that is pleasing to the Lord; that makes her a good woman. She watches over the affairs of her household, loves her children and her husband.

Chapter V

Satan's Most Dangerous Weapon (Woman)

The first of those weapons that satan used on man was Eve. Indirectly, the devil used the serpent to get to the man. The serpent was envious of man which made its plot his downfall. What the devil did was to the serpent to attack the mind of the woman with his subtle, clever, mischievous, and with his most dangerous weapon of cunning. The gliding stealthy movement of the serpent is a fitting symbol of the insidious progress of temptation. The woman guileless and unsuspecting falls the trap. The serpent had woven a spell on the woman. The woman with her beautiful eyes looked upon the tree with a new longing.

> "And when (refers to time) the woman saw that the tree was good for food, and that it was pleasant to the eyes, and a tree to be desired to make one wise; she took of the fruit thereof,

and did eat: and she gave also unto her husband
with her, and he did eat." (Genesis 3:6 KJV)

Once the man ate of the fruit, God called the man into
question. Because of the woman, man lost his home in the
Garden of Eden; also she made man's work harder.

"And unto Adam He said: Because thou hast
hearkened unto the voice of thy wife, and hast
eaten of the tree, of which I commanded thee,
saying; thou shalt not eat of it, cursed is the
ground for thy sake; in sorrow shalt thou eat
of it all the days of thy life; thorns also thistles
shall it bring forth to thee; and thou shalt eat
the herb of the field. In the sweat of thy face
shalt thou eat bread, till thou return unto the
ground; for out of it wast thou taken; for dust
thou art, and unto dust shalt thou return."
(Genesis 3:17-19 KJV)

The man was born immortal; but when he ate the forbidden
fruit, God said, "Thou shalt surely die"; i.e., thou must
inevitably become mortal. While this explanation removes
the difficulty that Adam and Eve lived a long time after
they had eaten of the forbidden fruit, it assumes that man
was created to be a deathless being. The devil used the
serpent to use the woman to bring the man down. The
devil also used the woman (Delilah) to bring down the
man (Samson):

"And it came to pass afterward, that he loved a
woman in the Valley of Sorek, whose name was
Delilah. And the lords of the Philistines came

up unto her and said unto her, Entice him, and see wherein his great strength lieth, and by what means we may prevail against him, that we may bind him to afflict him: and we will give thee every one of us eleven hundred pieces of silver." (Judges 16:4-5 KJV)

Now this was the second time that Samson was enticed by a woman and lost a lot. First by his own wife:

"And it came to pass on the seventh day, that they said unto Samson's wife, Entice thy husband, that he may declare unto us the riddle, lest we burn thee and thy Father's house with fire: have ye called us to take that we have? Is it not so? (Judges 14:15 KJV)

Samson gave into his wife when he was not supposed to tell her the secret which God has given him.

"And Samson's wife wept before him, and said, thou dost but hate me, and lovest me not: thou hast put forth a riddle unto the children of my people, and hast not told it me. And he said unto her, behold, I have not told it my Father nor my mother, and shall I tell it thee? And she wept before him the seven days, while their feast lasted; and it came to pass on the seventh day that he told her, because she lay sore upon him: and she told the riddle of the children of her people." (Judges 14:16, 17 KJV)

Because of that he lost his wife to his companion:

> "But Samson's wife was given to his companion, whom he had used as his friend." (Judges 14:20 KJV)

After Samson lost his wife, there was another woman that seemed to be the love of his life.

> "And it came to pass afterward, that he loved a woman in the Valley of Sorek, whose name was Delilah. And the Lords of the Philistines came up unto her, and said unto her, Entice him, and see where his great strength lieth, and by what means we may prevail against him, that we may bind him to afflict him: and we will give thee every one of us eleven hundred pieces of silver." (Judges 16:4-5 KJV)

The devil is still using the weapon he used in Genesis in the Garden of Eden. Just as you will load a gun with shells, he loads the woman with cunning deceptions. The devil is seeking to find out the strength of the man, to bring him down.

> "And Delilah said to Samson, tell me, I pray thee, where in thy great strength lieth, and wherewith thou mightest be bound to afflict thee." (Judges 16:6 KJV)

Delilah with her beautiful self, pretty eyes, and pretty lips speaking with rejection on her pretty rounded face, pressed him until he gave in.

> "And it came to pass, when she pressed him daily with her words, and urged him, *so* that

his soul was vexed unto death; That he told her
all his heart, and said unto her, There hath not
come a razor upon mine head; for I have been
a Nazarite unto God from my mother's womb:
if I be shaven, then my strength will go from
me, and I shall become weak, and be like any
other man. (Judges 16:16-17 KJV)

This proves that God doesn't want a weak man. When
Delilah realized that Samson had confided in her, she put
him to sleep on her knees. Then she called in a man, and
had him cut off the seven locks of hair on Samson's head.
She began to weaken him, and his strength left him. The
sad part is he did not know that his God given strength
had left him. It was a woman that brought big-old Samson
down. The Philistines seized him and gouged out his eyes.
They brought him down to Gaza and bound him in bronze
fetters. He became a grinder in prison (for example, Exodus
11:5; 12:29 KJV). Because of the woman, Samson lost his
eyes and his position with God.

The destructive, effects of deceit and quarreling on
personal relationships is exemplified tragically in the story
of Delilah and Samson. It also demonstrates graphically
how the word "love" can be used in a relationship which
reveals no indication that love exists at all. Samson was
apparently drawn primarily by sexual attraction, and
Delilah showed no concern for his welfare when offered
money to betray him. Relationships based on feelings
such as these have little chance for survival. Only faithful
commitment can overcome conflicts and competing
loyalties.

It was a woman that caused King Ahab his life:

> "And the word of the Lord came to Elijah the
> Tishbite, saying, arise, go down to meet Ahab
> king of Israel, which is in Samaria: behold,
> he is in the vineyard of Naboth, where he is
> gone down to possess it. And thou shalt speak
> unto him saying, thus saith the Lord, hast
> thou killed, and also taken possession? And
> thou shalt speak unto him saying, thus saith
> the Lord, in the place where dogs licked the
> blood of Naboth, shall dogs lick thy blood,
> even thine!" (I Kings 21:17-19)

King Ahab was charged with murder and taken into
possession, because his wife caused him to sell himself
to evil. In the Book of Revelation, there are visions and
symbols which carry the same character as the first woman
that has been tricked by the devil; such as, "The Great
Whore"; the great persecuting power, whose destruction had
been foretold; called by this name on account of her awfully
corrupting influence; sitteth upon many water; ruleth over
many nations to bring them down.

Hath committed fornication; by their idolatrous devotion to
her service; made drunk with the wine of her fornication; an
allusion to the wine-cup which harlots give to their deluded
votaries. The meaning is that the inhabitants of the earth
have been deluded, corrupted and made wretched by her
errors, vices and control.

A woman; representing this idolatrous persecuting power,
who with all deceivableness of unrighteousness, by pretended

miracles, shows, splendid decoration, indulgences, jubilees and blandishments or various sorts, had been deceiving and enslaving the nations, promising all good to those who should follow, and all evil to those who should oppose her. (II Thessalonians 2:9-12; I Timothy 4:1-3 KJV) Notice that same spirit that the devil put in the serpent and the serpent used it on the woman. This same spirit is used here in the Book of Revelation to bring down the nation.

Purpose-scarlet-gold-and pearls - indicating her vast wealth and luxury, and the gorgeous and splendid decorations, by which she dazzled and captivated the deluded multitude.

Mystery - apparently indicating the symbolic character of her name.

Drunken with blood – expressive of the vast multitude whom she, by her inquisitions, wars ad in various other ways had cause to be put to death, because they would not yield to her seductions.

CHAPTER VI

THE POWER OF THE WOMAN'S BEAUTY

When God made the woman and brought her to man, he looked and saw the most beautiful creature he had ever seen, and that he became a poet, he states:

> "And Adam said, 'This is now bone of my bones, and flesh of my flesh; she shall be called Woman because she was taken out of Man."
> (Genesis 2:23 KJV)

Jacob was over taken with the beauty of Rachel:

> "And Laban had two daughters: the name of the elder was Leah, and the name of the younger was Rachel. Leah was tender eyed; but Rachel was beautiful and well favoured."
> (Genesis 29:16, 17 KJV)

Jacob did love Rachel, she was beautifully formed (shape) and fair to look upon, that he will work seven years for her.

After seven years Jacob did not get Rachel, because Laban said:

> ". . . it must not be so done in our country, to give the younger before the first-born. Fulfil her week, and we will give thee this also for the service which thou shalt serve with me yet seven other years." (Genesis 29:26-27 KJV)

Then Jacob worked fourteen years for Rachel; she still was beautifully formed and fair to look upon. Laban gave Jacob Rachel eight days after marrying Leah, on the understanding that Jacob was to serve Laban for another seven years. After the giving of the Law at Sinai, the marrying of two sisters was forbidden.

It was the beauty of Bathsheba that brought King David down. One day in the Spring, the warm spring air, all the other Kings went off to war, but David stayed back. One evening David got up from his bed and walked around on the roof of the palace. From the roof, he saw a woman bathing. She was **very** beautiful. The beauty of her entire body took him that he sent someone to find out about her. The beauty of Bathsheba caused David to arrange the death of Bathsheba's husband, Uriah. David's desire for Bathsheba caused him to ignore God's Law. A sexual relationship outside of marriage is sin. No office or position exempts a person. Adultery was forbidden by Hebrew law. (Exodus 20:14; Leviticus 20:10 KJV) Because of the beauty of Bathsheba, David brought the wrath of God down upon himself. David and Bathsheba had both suffered the wrath of God in the death of the child born from their adulterous relationship.

Look what the power of the beauty of the woman did to the man. But still no one has the moral right to take something just because the power to do so is available. Her beauty can trap men. The Book of Proverbs states:

> "For the commandment is a lamp; and the law is light; and reproofs of instruction are the way of life: to keep thee from the evil woman, from the flattery of the tongue of a strange woman. Lust not after her beauty in thine heart; neither let her take thee with her eyelids." (Proverbs 6:23-25 KJV)

The evil woman; must represent mankind's physical desires, don't make a huge mistake and get trapped. Among tragedies is the disaster of sexual sins with immoral woman and wayward wives. Such sin begins with flirtatious looks and ends with disastrous punishment. Shame, disgrace and revenge chart life's course for the adulterer. As the serpent trapped Eve with his speech, so women would trap men with their speech.

> "With her much fair speech she caused him to yield, with the flattering of her lips she forced him. He goeth after her straightway, as an ox goeth to the slaughter, or as a fool to the correction of the stocks; Till a dart strike through his liver; as a bird hasteth to the snare, and knoweth not that it is for his life." (Proverbs 7:21-23 KJV)

She turns him from the righteous path. She sways him with her deftness, turns him aside with her slick talk. Suddenly, he follows after her on his own making further enticements on the part of the evil inclination unnecessary. He followed her on the spur of the moment, against his better judgment. This is why he moves haltingly like the ox when led to the slaughter house. He is hesitant until the arrow of passion pierces his liver. He is like a bird that hurries to the trap not knowing it will cost it its life.

The beauty of Abraham's wife, Sarai caused him to lie. (Genesis 12:10-13 KJV) Sarai was very beautiful; she was then in middle age and apparently had retained her youthful beauty. In verses 14-15 (KJV) it states:

> "And it came to pass, that, when Abram was come into Egypt, the Egyptians beheld the woman that she was very fair. The princes also of Pharaoh saw her, and commended her before Pharaoh: and the woman was taken into Pharaoh's house."

Beauty cannot be hidden. It has power to cause trouble. Just as Abraham, if you marry a beautiful woman, it can even cost your life, because men don't respect another man, that's if he sees and desires your beautiful wife. As Abraham got in trouble because of a beautiful woman, so did David. The Bible states:

> "And it came to pass in an evening tide, that David arose from off his bed, and walked upon the roof of the king's house: and from the roof he saw a woman washing herself; and the woman was very beautiful to look upon." (II Samuel 11:2 KJV)

At nightfall, David rose from his bed, after his afternoon rest and took a stroll around the roof of the palace. He saw a woman bathing on the roof, and she was very beautiful. She was cleaning herself of her menstrual impurity. The roof of David's palace was presumably higher than most, where David could look down on the City roofs. She was the wife of another man. But her beauty caused David to kidnap her. David sent messengers to bring her as Abimelcck's kidnapping of Sarai (Genesis 20:2 KJV). Her beauty caused David to become an adulterer and a murderer. The result is the woman became pregnant. These are the only words Bathsheba spoke during the whole affair. Remember, it happens all because of the beauty of the woman. There is power in beauty.

Chapter VII

The Experiences of a Young Black Boy in the Woods (World) with These Beautiful Creatures

With these beautiful creatures this story begins one late spring day with me and my friend Allen. Allen has been my friend for a long time; we even dated twin girls before. They would only stay home because their parents were strict. We could only see them when their parents were home. While we talked, the parents were nearby in the other room. Well, I was 14 going on 15 and my buddy Allen was about two years older than I. Ok, back to my story.

There was some talk about some Jews going up-state to New York to live, and workers were needed to build whatever! We had never been out of Baltimore MD, so Allen said to me, "Let's go up there!" We had a little job, so Allen said let's quit and go. I let him talk me into it. I guess we had less than a hundred dollars between us. The bus tickets were about $6 each. Well it was about in the year 1955 or 1956. We left and didn't let our parents know. I thought about that after a year or two later, that was wrong, well I was only a boy thinking I was a man at that time. Well, we are on the bus "Trailway", beautiful red, sitting near the window with the window down; I felt the warm spring breeze. Riding out of the City, I began to see trees, green grass, mountains and farm lands. The bus would stop and we ate. Finally, we got to the big city of New York. Those New York buildings were the tallest I have ever seen. We had to catch another bus to carry us to upstate New York to South Fallsburg. So we rode, the bus stopped again and we ate, but when we got to South Fallsburg we were out of money, as they say "we were broke."

South Fallsburg was a small town and in about five-ten minutes you could walk from one end of town to the other. It looked like one of those old cowboy towns. Only one Sheriff in town and seemed like one of everything, one movie theater and one diner called "David's Diner." We will talk about David's Diner later. Well, now we have no money and we are hungry. It was about noon and we knew no one. We are now very hungry!

After getting off the bus, we didn't know where to go. We were told when we get to New York, find Reverend Smith, "a preacher" who had a boarding house. We went into this bar and no one was there except the bartender. He was an old man, bald on top with hair around the sides, an old Jewish man. We talked for a while, no one was there but us. A little while later a couple of workers came in for lunch. Wow, that food smelled good! I think one of the men was watching me stir-down his food, so he brought me a plate of bake beans and two franks (hotdogs); up there they call them "franks." They did not buy anything for my friend. I guess because I was the youngest. Those bake beans were good, and those franks were big and good. It was a shame that I did not give my friend any, but he hitched one of my franks anyway and laughed. After eating, we were told where Reverend Smith lived. We were not too far from where he lived. He was a barber also and I believe he cut hair for $3.75. He told us that we could stay there until we get a job. We were in one of those cheaper rooms, where there were three or four small beds, lined-up as in a hallway.

Early in the morning, some Jewish men came by to pick-up laborers. They would pick up everyone except me. Maybe it was because I was too young. One day I had $.10 in my pocket and my friend and I went to that same bar again. I don't know if it was our second or third time there, and I still don't know how we were eating. But this time when we went into the Bar, I saw a sign that said, "Chicken Dinners - $.10", and that was all I had in my pocket. I said to that old Jewish man, "Give me a chicken dinner", while my friend was standing there watching. The Jewish man placed a napkin on the table in front of me, and then he reached and got the salt and pepper shakers and placed them beside the napkin. Then he turned around, reached and got something and turned back to me again, slammed his hand down on the counter in front of me, raised his hand and there was an egg. "That was my chicken dinner!"

Those around me laughed; it wasn't funny because I was hungry.

Well, I don't know how long it took but I got a job. Reverend Smith had three or two sons; well one was a drunk and he loved to drink wine. He would do day's work, but this particular day he was too drunk to go so he took me. This was my first time meeting Mr. Richman. He was about 62 years old with gray thin hair. He drove me up town to this place and I have never ever seen anyplace like it. There was a big white house and that is where Mr. Richman and his wife lived. There was another big and long building where there was a restaurant on one side, and in the back was a place where they danced and played games. Between the big white house and the building was a big swimming pool. Further in back of them were twenty small buildings called "Bungalow." I worked all day and his wife fed me. She asked me what was it that I liked to eat. I said bread and jelly with milk to drink. That was good! Still being a boy but thinking I was a man. Well, that day came to an end and Mr. Richman drove me home. But he liked me, so he gave me another job with his friend not too far from his place, just about ten minutes away further up the hill. A place called, "The White Rose Hotel." The next day I was picked up by Mr. Richman's friend. I can't think of his name; that's a shame, but when we pulled up to his driveway from off the road, we still had a good ways to go up the hill. That was the biggest white house I had ever seen with so many rooms.

Now I was beginning to learn some Jewish cultures. My job was a "Bell Hop", one who carries the luggage when the guest arrive and leave, along with some other work around the hotel. Well by this time, I no longer lived with Reverend Smith. I now stayed at the hotel having my own room. I don't know whether or not I ever paid Reverend Smith. I learned how to earn money. I would talk to the male guest and make them feel more important than they really were. Then they would give me more money than expected. Then I met a Jewish girl and we became friends. I was 14, going on 15 and she was 13 years old. I found out that someone was noticing us when this man who was eating in the hotel lobby wanted to sell me a girl's angle bracelet. I said, "No." He replied and said, "Buy it for your girlfriend." I didn't buy it; we were just friends.

Now I was 15 and the girls really began to look very beautiful to me, as the hot summer began to fill the streets and roads, and the hotels and bungalows. There was a crowd of young people, girls and boys. I began to learn and live the ways of the Jewish teenagers. I had not seen my friend Allen now in about a month, because I no longer lived in town and I didn't go downtown.

At this hotel, "The White Rose Hotel", I began to be very friendly with many teenagers around my age who were staying at the hotel. As I said before, the hotel had a large swimming pool and inside of the hotel there was a small room, as of a Disk Jockey Studio room, with a microphone and loud speakers that sat on the outside of the hotel. I decided one day to just pick up the mic and sing. When I did, I became a star around the hotel. I would sing Nat King Cole's songs in the day to the adults, and one song that I loved to sing was, "Looking Back over My Life." When I finished singing, I would walk out around and down to the pool, and some of the people would say, "Were you the one singing?" With a smile I'd say yes, and at night I would sing to the teenagers. They all gathered around and listened to me while I sang Elvis Presley songs. The one I loved to sing best of Elvis's songs was "Love Me Tender." Oh yes, by the way, I would also play my guitar.

One late summer day, probably around late August, there was a place not far from The White Rose Hotel, but still on the property, where we gathered there all summer. I was the only Negro boy there; but, it didn't matter because they didn't treat me different from them. We had lots of fun doing what teenagers do. I really befriended this group of Jewish boys and girls. Here I experienced a strange thing in life that I never felt before. I was so attached to these Jewish girls and boys that I felt I was a part of them or something greater. That late summer day, I watched those girls and boys climb into this 1956 convertible olds mobile, red and white, with the top down leaving The White Rose Hotel going down the road that exits the hotel onto the main highway. As I watched, something seemed to be taken away from me. I felt that I had lost everything that was inside of me. I knew I would never see them again. The place, "The White Rose Hotel", didn't matter to me anymore. I didn't know that love could do that to a person. If it was love, it was the first time in my life that I felt like that. Even to this day, I can still see them fading out of my sight. I wished that I could see them again. Well, around the hotel everything seemed dead. Most everyone was gone back to the City.

The Jews would come up from the City of New York with their family when school closed and would return after Labor Day Monday. I also would come back to my home in Baltimore and go back to school.

I remembered that before I had met the group of young people that I just mentioned above, when I first got to The White Rose Hotel, my job was a Bell Hop among other things. I was blessed (by God) to have the gift of relating to people. When people first came to the hotel, I would meet them at their car and take their luggage up to their room and they would give me tips. This one person I could really sweet talk him. I would make him feel real important, and he would show off and give me more money. He would travel back and forth to the City while his family would stay at the hotel. He had one child, a little girl about three or four years of age.

I loved dancing. I always danced for as long as I can remember. One mid-summer day while sitting in the lobby of the White Rose Hotel, not many guests were there except my Jewish girlfriend and this young man about who looked about in his early or mid-twenties, and his wife about the same age. They were playing music. "Can you dance", she asked? I replied, "yes." It was a fast song, just what I liked to dance to. So we danced, and danced. I took her by the hand and swung her around, twisting our feet, just laughing and having a wonderful time. When the song was over, the next song came on and she said she wanted to dance again. "No", I said! "Why", she asked? "It's a slow song", I replied, knowing that a negro boy does not dance slow with a white girl in the early 50's, not what you call "the two-step." "That's a slow song", I said, and she replied, "Can we dance to that?" "That's a two-step dance", I said. "Let's dance", she replied. Her husband responded to that and said, "Are you crazy?" Boy, he didn't like that, and that was the end of that! I don't think that I really saw them anymore.

I had mentioned before that I loved Tony Curtis movies. This one night I walked down town to the Theater in South Fallsburg. I watched the movie called "Something of Value", staring Rock Hudson and Sidney Poitier. When I got back that night, a couple of Jewish girls were sitting in the lobby and the lobby was kind of dark. They seemed to be sad about something. "What's the matter," I asked? They replied, "We had to stay here and babysit"; "Where you been", they asked me? "To the movies", I said! Oh, that's where we wanted to go; believe it or not! I acted out the part of Sidney Poitier in front of them and they were so happy the rest of the night. As I stated before, all my close friends had left. So I did find a few friends just down the hill and across the road from the White Rose Hotel. We mostly met in the evenings playing music and partying. That was during the time when a new record came out called, "Sixteen Candle." I had never experienced this kind of fund before. Back home I was dancing when the family was having a party and they would call me to come and dance. I loved dancing, but I was doing it for them, but now I was doing it to enjoy myself with my friends, girls and boys.

Well the main idea of this story is women. If I have not already told you, that the first time that I really felt my body,

(Maybe I'm not putting it into the right meaning of what I want to say.) needed to be around or connected to, or with a female. This young Jewish girl about 13, I was about 15 and we became close friends. We would run around inside the hotel playing, and one day an old Jewish man was selling some jewelry; earrings, necklaces, etc. I told him I didn't want to buy anything; but I didn't notice him watching me, because his reply was, "Buy it for your girlfriend." He wanted me to buy an angel bracelet for her. I don't think I did.

Well the season was ending and the summer was fading fast. All of my friends were gone. There were little cabinets near the hotel where the Negro help would stay. There was a knock at my door, and there stood a young black boy. The first other black person I had seen since I had been there. Since all my friends had left, I didn't go out much. He was telling me that there was an Indian girl that was in one of the cabins who was a "help." She wouldn't open the door to let me talk to her.", he said. It was late that evening toward dust dark. After that, I never saw him again. But he told me which cabin the girl was in. I thought that I'd go and talk with her, feeling confident that I could. I felt that I could talk to any woman and win her. I watched a lot of Tony Curtis moves, how he would talk to woman and win them over. I even tried to wear my hair like him. One day while at the hotel, I went to her cabin, knocked a couple of times on the door and she came to the door and cracked it open just enough to see me. After a few minutes I talked her into a date.

On the next day, mid-day sunny and warm, I went to her cabin and she was ready. She was so beautiful; beautiful brownish tan with black hair, seemed to be tied up in a ball above her head. We walked from the hotel down the road on to the main road. I didn't have a car, but it didn't matter because I didn't have a driver's license. We walked in the nice summer breeze. Butterflies were flying around; the sky was of blue color with white clouds. The grass was green with yellow dandelions, which seemed to be everywhere. I reached down and picked one up and gave it to her while smiling, and she began to smile. I felt that I needed to get romantic, so I looked starring at her saying let your hair down. "Why", she said refusing to do so? I began to show displeasure on my face. She looked at me and it seemed that she liked me. She began to reach and take her hair loose, and it fell down pass her shoulders. Oh, what a beautiful sight to see! She knew I liked it, so she smiled. I began to forget about my other friend. We walked until we got near the town. Just about a half mile before we reached town, we saw an old friend, George and his girlfriend sitting in the yard. "Where are you going", he asked? "Into town at David's Diner", I said. "Can we go", he asked? I replied, "Yes come on." He and his girlfriend joined us and we finally reached David's Diner. After we had eaten, we got up and I left a $.50 tip. I was showing off. As we were walking out from the table where we were sitting, George turned and went back. I thought he had left something, his hat or something; but, he really went and got the tip that I had left. George was not really a friend. I had only seen him about twice. There were only a few Negros living in up State New York at that time. The Jews had just started coming up; they were building and they needed some laborers. All of the Negros lived near the township. After we left David's Diner, I never saw

George again. We, this beautiful girl and I, walked back to her place. I walked her to the door, but she didn't let me in. We said good night and that was the last I saw her.

At the end of the season, we were ready to go home. The friends that were left with me from Baltimore were Allen, Richard and Gogle. I had saved some money to take back home with me. I put it inside of my guitar and I forgot it when I let one of my friends use it. When I got it back, my money was gone. I never asked them, so I never got it back. Therefore, I had to stay a couple of months to earn more money. Allen and I got a job at some bungalow just a few miles away from South Frostburg.

I was no longer at this time staying with Mr. Richman. I was now back at the boarding house with the preacher. This was my first time with all Negro friends. Life seemed altogether different. We would go to the club and get drunk, not me, but them. We created a small gang called, "The B-More", because we all were from Baltimore. We wore black pants and red sweaters with a white pearl earring in our left ear. Wherever we went people were afraid of us. We didn't do anything dangerous; they were just afraid of us because they heard so much about Baltimore City. We mostly went out at night; everything was happening at night. This one night, one of my friends met a beautiful Negro girl from California. She had a beautiful blue '54 or '55 Ford. We all got into her car, me and my three friends Allen, Richard and Gogle. We drove a long way, maybe about an hour drive. We arrived at a big club with many people. She seemed like a high class person. She was very beautiful with a high complexion with long black or blackish brown hair. I was the youngest of the crowd. I didn't even get a chance to dance with her; all I could do was watch. It was bad, or not right in my sight to be so young at that time. It seemed that I was missing everything. With my Jewish friends, it didn't seem like you had to be that old, or maybe it was the life that was different.

This season ended with this great night remembering this beautiful black girl about twenty-two years old, and I'm about fifteen. But, still it was a good way to end my season here up State New York, at South Frostburg. The summer was now ended and I went back home to Baltimore. Well, back to school with lots of wonderful memories.

After the school season was over, I traveled back to up State New York alone. When I got the opportunity to go to Fallsburg New York, I went back to the preacher's boarding house and there Mr. Richman picked me up and said this time I will be working for him. He had three sons, two were married with family and one, Joey, was married but with no children. Joey loved to party, so he was no help to his father at all. The other two were, or seemed business minded; but they would go back and forth to the City, so they were not any help also. Do you believe what Mr. Richman did? He made me, and I mean he made me, to be in charge over his business as far as the bungalows was concerned. There were about nearly twenty bungalows on the property. I had to cut the grass; I had a riding mower and also had to clean the large swimming pool every day. If anything got broken in the bungalows, I was responsible for seeing that it was fixed. I was also in charge of the vendors. God had blessed me at a young age. Mr. Richman had a granddaughter named Betty; she and I were really close. I was about one or two years older than she was. She had dark brown hair, and she had a baby sister named Faye who had blonde hair. She also had a middle sister, but I never really got her name. Betty had a really good personality. We were so close that Mr. Richman thought that I might become his grandson-in-law. He wanted to send me to the Rabbi School, but it didn't happen.

My second year in South Fallsburg was beautiful. There were two young girls from the City of New York who came down with their parents for the summer. We would dance and they really loved the way I danced. One of them was named Gloria. She had beautiful brown hair with brown eyes, and the other one named Darlene had dark brown hair. I liked Gloria better. I mostly danced with Gloria; once or twice I danced with both at the same time, but my choice was Gloria. I taught her how to dance and when she went back to the City, the following year or season when we meet, she told me that she had won an award for dancing. While we were having fun in the back of the concession part of the building, Betty was working. She had to work because her grandparents owned the place.

From where Mr. Richman's place was, the distance to downtown was about a 15 minute walk. The first friend I met lived downtown where the preacher's boarding house was located. He was a white non-Jewish boy about my age. He loved fishing and hunting. We did not meet often because I stayed or spent much of my time with the Jewish boys and girls that had a group called "The Crazy Cat Club." This friend that I'm talking about is Alvin. One day he took me to his house and he had lots of guns and rifles. We would sometimes go deep up into the mountains at night and shoot big rats.

One day in the evening we were in town and we stopped at a pool hall. In the pool hall were only Negros and Alvin was the only white boy. We were playing pool and somehow something went wrong that lead Alvin and I against each other. Maybe I let myself favor the Negros. I hit Alvin across his head with my cue stick. "If you were in the South, you wouldn't do that", he said, and walked out. I stayed in the pool hall until late that night. Somewhere maybe about midnight, Alvin came back and tapped on the big window of the pool hall and beaconed me to come out. I went out and he asked me, "Let's go up and shoot some rats. "Okay", I replied! Just at that moment, that little dispute that we had had been forgotten. We went to his house and got the rifles and went up through the dark night into the woody mountains. Sometimes I walked in front of him and sometimes he walked in front of me. He was one of the best friends I ever had. A few years after that when I went into the army and had come back, I was told that Alvin had drowned while out fishing, one of the things he loved to do.

This is my second year in up State New York and I'm now working for Mr. Richman. I am a year older and now a member of the Crazy Cats Club. We would go around at night, jumping into swimming pools at other hotels. We didn't use drugs, or drank any hard liquor. We would buy a quart of beer and use a straw to suck the beer through the straw. That's how we got our high; we didn't need much. That was enough to make us run around and jump the fences into other pools. In the day, we would go to a place called Echo Lake. That was like a beach and many people would go to swim, eat and suntan there. It was a beautiful lake. I could hold my breath about two minutes, I would lay on a rock in the shallow water as the sun would shine down off my body, and when I saw certain girls go out into the water, I would slide off the rock into the water underneath the surface, swimming under the water, to where the girl was and then swim back to the rock. We would do that for most of the day.

Some days early in the morning, I would go to another place where one of Mr. Richman's sons was staying. I would go there early in the morning and find Betty still in bed. I would surprise her by catching her in bed with Noxzema covered over her face and she would try to pull the cover over her face when she saw me. We laughed; we were really close. I remember her always wearing a blue dress. Well, it seemed like most of the time. Maybe it was because I liked seeing her in blue. We spent a lot of time together that year; a lot of time talking, laughing and working in the confectionary part of the hall. This one early summer morning, a slight breeze went blowing through the air passing my face, while I was cleaning the swimming pool, just at the gate exit of the pool, as I stood with black pants and white shirt with the first button opened at the chest, my hair combed the way Tony Curtis wore his with that little piece down his forehead, I saw through the early morning a little figure of a young girl coming towards me with her hands to her mouth. When she had gotten close to me, she was shaky with beautiful brown hair and about 13 or 14 years old. "What's the matter", I asked. "You might laugh", she replied. "No, I will not", I said. She let her hands down and her lips were swollen. "Something bit me", she said. I took her in my arms, she laid on my chest as her long hair laid on my arms. I comforted her and spoke kind words to her. She felt my care for her and she was encouraged. She went away happy. Somehow, I felt that there was something special about the female species; that's if I should use that word. I guess that I'm saying that there is a need for me to study women. There was something about each one that I met.

There was one girl that I only saw once, as I was going up the steps to go into the Concession Store, I stepped right in front of her; "Little bird mouth", I said to her. She had the most beautiful little red lips. She smiled and said to me, "You have curly eye lashes." Women wished to have my eyelashes. There were so many different kinds of women; of all colors and sizes, eyes, faces, hair, mouth or lips and bodies. Everywhere you would look, there they were. Then I wondered how and why did God make women so beautiful. Their voices so soft and produces a lovely sound. One day when I was painting near the second floor window of Mr. Richman's house, I was singing a song called "The Wayward Wind." As I was singing, I heard a lovely voice through the window, joining me as I sang the song. That was one of the greatest feelings I had in my early life. I could barely see her through the window, but I waited for her to come down as

I stood outside waiting to see her. She came down and came out of the door, she was beautiful, black hair with a white blouse and black pants on. She was about twenty-five years old; I was about sixteen, but yet she was Joey's girlfriend or wife who was Mr. Richman's youngest son. But she gave me a lovely smile. It made me feel like she loved me. I took another job at David's Dinner. After working for Mr. Richman until 4 pm, I went to work for David at the Dinner until 2 am in the morning. I believe my hours were from 6 pm to 2 am in the morning at David's Dinner. My job was working in the kitchen, in the back of the restaurant peeling potatoes, and etc. I met two white friends there that was working at the counter serving. It was a married couple about in their mid-twenties. After I got to know Mr. David, who was the owner, he let me come down in the basement with him and some of the other older men. They would plan to bet on horses that raced at Monticello. I found out that they were holding out, maybe they were cheating because they had sheets of paper, looking at horses and studying the horses by name.

Sometimes, about 2 am in the morning when I got off, I would stay around because the night clubs close at those big hotels and many of those entertainers would come to David's Dinner to eat breakfast. This is how I found out about the many different ways to order eggs, sunny-side up, over easy, etc. but I like my eggs scrambled with ketchup. I also learned to put ketchup on my eggs from David's Dinner. I learned a lot listening to those entertainers who were singers, dancers and comedians. I began to feel like a big shot, whatever that is, but it felt good being with them.

My best times were in the day with Mr. Richman, Betty and my Jewish friends there.

It was another beautiful summer, but now it was coming to an end. Once again, Labor Day was past and most of the Jewish families were going back to the big city, New York City, New York. So, now I'm getting ready to go back home to go to school. This one evening before I was getting ready to leave, I met a white boy about my age that was from Monticello, New York where the race was. Somehow I met him downtown as we were walking towards Mr. Richman's house where I was staying. For whatever reason I don't know, but as we were walking we met two young Jewish girls about our age. One had dark brown hair, for it was late evening and we could barely see, and one had blond hair. She was called Chickie. As we walked, they were walking behind us. We, my friend and I, were trying to find out which one was going to be our date for the night. Well, after while we found out that we didn't have to figure that out, because Chickie had already done so. "I don't want vanilla, I want chocolate", she said. So Chickie was my date for that night and also the last for the season up in Up-State New York. I caught the bus and went back home.

My final year in South Fallsburg, New York back with Mr. Richman. All the same boys and girls were back at Mr. Richman's bungalows in the summer breeze. Lots of dancing, swimming, laughing, music and fun. Now the season once again had come to an end. This time, Mr. Richman said, "I paid taxes, you just as well stay here and go to school." So, that I did. Now the fall season was different than the spring and summer seasons. Now, instead of working, I was in school. There were about two of us Negro boys in the whole school. The name of the school was "South Fallsburg High." They had a soccer team. I went out for the soccer team and made the team, but I didn't make the first string team. I never got to play in the games, but I learned to play during practice. I still remember one early fall evening after school there was a practice. Most all the Jewish boys would drive their car to school, or maybe it was their father's car. So, I went back home, to Mr. Richman's place where I was staying, from school and found the keys to Mr. Richman's 54 or 55 Buick and drove to school showing off. After practice, on my way back to Mr. Richman, I passed Mr. Richman walking with his wife and other Jews. On Friday at 6 pm, they walked. It's the Jewish custom. When I passed Mr. Richman, I looked back through the rear view mirror and Mr. Richman was shaking his finger at me. I was afraid, but when he got home, he didn't say a word to me. I would get the school bus every day from in front of Mr. Richman's house to go to school. Maybe with all the stops we will get to the school in about 30-35 minutes.

This one particular beautiful fall morning, while waiting for the bus, Sandria, a beautiful girl that lived not too far from us rode pass and stopped. "You want a ride", she asked? "Yes", I replied. I got in and she drove off, just her and I. Later, I felt real good about myself, because she was so pleased to have me in her car. She drove past her girlfriends, waved and smiled at them. I think that she was showing off. I also believed that she was supposed to have picked them up. Every year I felt myself growing into a need to be around beautiful girls (women). They began to be everywhere. Maybe I'm trying to say, why did God put so many beautiful women in the world, of all colors, of hair, eyes and shapes? They are dangerous when they attack with their beauty.

One day I was sitting in class behind this one girl and when I looked up, she was watching me through her little hand mirror. This was my first Spanish class. Then it seemed to me that I had something that these female creatures wanted. I don't know what, but it seems like they are being drawn to me. Now the winter months had set in. It was now October; the weather was cold; what a great change from the Spring and Summer months at Mr. Richman's. All the Jewish people that were at Mr. Richman's has gone back to the City of New York. For the first time now, I am able to see how the Jews lived, which had settled here in South Fallsburg, New York. We are in school, and now it is near Halloween. For the first time in my life, I never could imagine how fun Halloween could be. The Senior Class had early dismissal that day for what you call a "Hay Ride." A tractor pulling a wagon with straw on the bed of the wagon. We sat or laid in the wagon on the straw. That night, we went to the school for a Halloween party. We had on our costume. Me and my buddy D.C., we called him D.C. because he was from Washington DC, were the only Negros in High School, but not in the same class. We both won the best costume outfit. We were dressed like Fidel Castro. Then I started to hang out with those Jewish boys and girls, the same way I did at Mr. Richman's. It was just like on T.V.; the rich parents would go to Florida for the weekend and leave their teenager at home. They would call their friends over, and we would have a wild party, I'm talking about wild. Some of us were upstairs, some downstairs, in the bed rooms, bathroom and everywhere. I have never had so much fun. Well, all good things must come to an end. Well just close to the closing of the school year recruiters came to the school and talked to all the seniors about going into the Military. My friend and I decided to go into the Military on that new program they have instead of four years, we volunteer for the two years. Well, my friend D.C. talked me into going as partners. So we ended up at White Hall, New York where we had to take tests all day long. By noon, I saw D.C and he gave me the thumbs-down meaning he did not make it. He had flat-feet, I think that is what it was called. Now he gets to go home and leaves me to go into the Military alone. After the day was finally over, I passed all the tests. Now all of us that passed were in one room to be sworn in. We all went to Coney Island. That was the place to go for fun. There was a beach, southwestern part of the borough of Brooklyn in New York City.

The next day, we were taken by buses to Fort Dix, New Jersey called the reception station, where we were fitted and given our army clothing such as; fatigues, and boots for training. Also dress clothes and sheets, the military style. We stayed in Fort Dix for about 30 days. We did not train there. We would get up early in the morning to go and eat, in the dining hall; we went for breakfast, lunch and dinner. Would you believe that we didn't have to pay a dime? This was not like when we first went to South Fallsburg, New York. We really had nothing to do, just walk around and eat. Maybe we were just waiting for our clothes that we were fitted for to come. I used to lie a lot, maybe because I was poor, and I tried to pretend that I was rich, but that I was somebody. I believe that I began to make some of the guys angry with me. I told them that I had a T-Bird back home. I was trying to make friends, but I found out that I couldn't make friends that way. Finally, our clothes came and we were given our clothing. We were told that we were going to leave Fort Dix, and we must pack our gear, then we were given a duffle bag. That day we packed our duffle bag because on tomorrow we were to catch a plane to Fort Benning Georgia. The next day we were ready, then they took us by trucks to the airport to catch the plane. I was excited by now at the age of nineteen, my first time on an airplane. We got on the plane and I had a window seat. This was a lot better than riding the bus, when we first went to New York. I could look down out of the window of the plane and see the farmland and the city at the same time. The sky and clouds were beautiful. As I sat, I felt the plane drop and catch itself. I was having fun. I don't know, but maybe we were in the air about three hours, maybe more. We got to Fort Benning Georgia about dusk dark. We landed at this big airport, and this big place, "building" was lit up and people were inside of it. I never saw a place like this. It was not like the airport where we caught the plane from Fort Dix. This place was a lot bigger and better. Our Lieutenant or Sergeant got us together and led us to the door, to go in because we were ready to eat. But the man on the other side of the door spoke, "They can't come in here", referring to us that were Negros. Our Lieutenant or Sergeant, I can't remember now which one it was, stood up for all of his men and I will never forget it for he was white.

Here in Fort Benning Georgia, we had about six weeks of hard training. We did push-ups, sit-ups and a whole lots of other exercises. We had some hard combat training. These army instructors were big and strong. They would show us first, how it was to be done. We didn't go anywhere; we had to stay on base. We learned to march and we would march for miles with a back pack and our rifle. That was really tough. We had a rifle called the M-1. Many of night, we would clean that M-1 after training all day. Then we would go into a big building with many tables and we would sit there, take that M-1 rifle apart completely and clean every part. After we clean it, we would oil it (each part), then put it back together. After about six weeks, we graduated. Then some of us went home, but some of us stayed and they sent us to Sand Hill Army Base just a few miles away; we went there by trucks. I was looking forward to going home, but I was one of the ones that they chose to stay.

The next six weeks were called AIT, some kind of advance training and it was harder than the first six weeks. They called the place Sand Hill because it was a lot of sand there. We did the same things we did the first six weeks, but harder. This time we were trained to do hand-to-hand combat. We would get up early in the morning and march with back packs and a rifle, and maybe about mid-night, we would stop and find a place to pitch tent. We would be so tired that we would just fall into the weeds and go to sleep. Sometimes when we would do that, strange things would happen. This one time, one of the soldiers was waiting by a bunch of fire ants that had bit him all over his body, and sometimes snakes would crawl in beside some of us to keep warm. The sergeants were to make men out of us by disciplining us.

There was a fellow there by the name of Harkin. He would always get into trouble. He was like the T.V. star, Gomer Pile. He was standing in line for inspection late one evening after training and once in line, we are not to move. But a mosquito landed on his face and he slapped it. The Sargent said to Harkin, "What are you doing?" Harkin said, "It was a mosquito!" The Sargent told Harkin to find the mosquito, so Harkin did find the mosquito. The Sargent made him dig a hole the size of a human grave and told Harkin to bury the mosquito. Harkin did just that. I believe it took him about 3-4 hours to do that.

The next hardest thing we were trained to do was to crawl under the machine gun's firing. We did lots of trial runs before we did the real thing. We would start in a pit and at night we would see the gun fire across the pit from where we were to climb out of. The gun fire was about 1 foot above the top of the pit, which we would climb out of. They would give us just a few seconds to climb quickly out of the pit before they start firing again. These were, I believe to be, 50th caliber machine guns, about four lined up in a row. After we got up out of the pit, we had to crawl about one hundred yards to the finish line. While we were crawling, there were explosives going off and smoke bombs. Then we had to crawl underneath barb wire that was about six inches off the ground, so we had to roll over on our backs and dig down into the ground with our helmets to get under the barb wire. That was our final big test.

The six weeks were drawing near. We, me and this big tall negro, decided to go downtown, but we didn't know where to go or what to do. We walked around until nearly mid-night. So we just walked until we ran into some M.P.'s (Military Police). I noticed them a good way down the street, so I told Greer, the big tall African American, that I mentioned before. Greer said, "Let us go through the alley." When we did, the M.P.'s were waiting for us. They took us and put us in some type of stockade, which is like a jail. A little small room with a toilet, and it was very dark inside. They took the string out of our shoes and took our belts. About 1 or 2 o'clock in the morning, my Sargent came and got me and told me to wait in the Chapel. I waited there until about 5 o'clock, and then he got me and took me to the mess hall, that's where soldiers eat. So, I peeled potatoes all that morning, until it was time for breakfast. I never did that again. I found out that I was put on "K.P" duty in the military. K.P. stands for kitchen patrol or kitchen police. It was used as a type of punishment in the past, but isn't commonly used in that manner in the modern military today. During my time there, I was training for the Airborne. Finally, we got a chance to go downtown; maybe about 5 or 6 of us. One of us was a Caucasian soldier and we were dressed in our military uniform. While walking downtown at high noon, on the main busy street, there were many cars and people; most of the people were Caucasian. We were in Georgia, in a town called Columbus. As we were walking all excited, I looked at the Caucasian soldier and his necktie was crooked. So, I reached with my hand to fix his necktie and it seemed that I was choking him. Cars were slamming their brakes all around us, so we quickly went to a window where clothes were being sold. When we got this Caucasian soldier to peep into the window at the clothes, we ran and left him; because, with him around, it seemed that we would be in trouble. We were glad to get out, but we didn't see any girls. We stayed in town until dusk dark, then we went to buy something to eat.

We saw this big bright building with a glass front and glass doors. The building was all lit up. I went to the door and reached for the handle, but one of the soldiers grabbed me and said, "Look there is a sign on the door." The sign on the door said "White Only-Color Around the Back." This was the year 1959. I had never seen anything like that before; so, we went around the back. There was a little small room, dark with a dim bulb and an old wooden bench. The room was about an 8' X 10', with a little sliding window connected to the main building. That was where the colored people would order their food. There was only one old colored lady sitting in there on the wooden bench. I believe that, that place was a bus station because we felt so bad how the colored people were being treated. When the bus came and this very old lady got on the bus, we felt like quitting the army and getting on the bus and ride away forever. But, somehow we didn't because I believed that we loved being a soldier.

The next time we went out we found a military barrack for female soldiers. We said one to the other, "Let's go in there and find someone." So we went inside and just as we went in, there sits a female soldier at a desk. We found out that all the girls were up in their rooms. So the girl at the desk said, "Who do you want to see?" We pretended that we knew one of the girls. She said, "What's her name?" There was a big board right beside her desk with a long list of names. So we picked one of the names, she smiled and looked at us for a while, and then she looked down on her desk and we followed her eyes down on the desk and the name we picked was her name. We laughed and rolled out of that building. Well, maybe we had about a few weeks lefH mentioned one day that if his parachute didn't come out, that he would jump on my back. Hawkins was in some ways like Gomer Pile, that old T.V. show. One day we were on the rifle range and on the rifle range we are to fire our weapon on command. It was something like, "Get ready, fire." But, Hawkins would fire his rifle on get ready every time; so the Lieutenant went and stood behind Hawkins to explain to him how to do it. The Lieutenant called Hawkins' name and Hawkins turned around with the rifle pointed right at the Lieutenant. The Lieutenant said, "Turn back around." Hawkins would do lots of crazy things, but one day we walked maybe about twenty-five miles with our pack on our back and our rifle. It began to get very heavy as we walked. Some of the soldiers were falling out and the Red Cross medical trucks would pick them up. I was so tired that in my mind I said I'm going to fall down just as some of the others did, but Hawkins came up behind me walking with strength and whistling as he was passing me. How could I let Hawkins out do me? When I saw Hawkins, then I gained strength and finished the journey. Now, there was something that I really didn't like, "guard duty"; it was four on and four off. That meant we had to watch for 4 hours and then someone would pick us up and we slept for 4 hours. Now I said we, which meant one at a time. That is, if someone is on duty at 8:00 pm, someone would have to relieve him at midnight. When I got picked up, I didn't know where I was going. Riding down this dark road at just before mid-night, all I could see was tall trees on either side. It seemed like we rode for about an hour. As we approached the place, I saw some lights. It was a little store. People were all around and I had said to myself, this is not bad, but a little while later, the cars started to leave one by one, and then there was one car. The lights were beginning to be cut off and finally, all the lights were out and the last car pulled away. Here I'm standing in the dark by myself. I didn't know what to do, but I'm a soldier getting ready for the Airborne. I looked behind me and discovered that I was standing in a grave yard, and behind the grave was a big and long dark barn. All my life as I was coming up, I didn't like grave yards. The folks had talked about the dead coming back to life, coming out of the grave. I started to go and hide under something, but something happened to me that night, deep down inside of me I was a soldier for the United States of America. I looked around myself and looked at the grave yard stones, and then I walked through the grave yard and walked around that big long barn. I'm a soldier. Someone came about 4 am and relieved me. I did many of the guard duties. After that, finally my time in George was ending. The final day that I was training for had come. I got my order for jump school in Kentucky, the "Screaming Eagles". But we didn't go to jump school because we turned down that order and volunteered to go to Germany. In Germany, the United States was in a cold war with Russia. So, we became the Gorillas, which was a new training for the way to fight in the Germany's woods, mountains and country.

Now I'm ready to board the plan to go home (Baltimore MD) to spend thirty days before going to Germany. I was a Private First Class, making about $78 (dollars) a month. I had never closed my bank account in New York at the Bank of Fallsburg. I had the Army to take money out of my pay every month. So, I went home and spend thirty days there. I met a young girl that I was dating before leaving to go to New York to board the big ship leaving for Germany. Before I left her, she gave me her ring. I was about 19 years old and she was about 17 years old.

I was told to go back to New York City to board the ship to Germany. I got on this big ship and went down into the bottom or a lower floor of the ship; that was where my bunk bed was. It seemed as though was hundredths of us on that ship. The officers with their families were on the upper decks. As we were leaving, I stood on the main deck level and watched the Statue of Liberty until it left my sight. Now all I could see was water and sky. I didn't know anyone on the ship, until about two or three days had past. The first day on the ship was very rough, not the water but learning to live on a ship. Some of the soldiers got sick and was vomiting even as we were at the table eating. It didn't bother me. Some of the soldiers had to take pills for sea sickness, because the ship was rocking so much. When on deck, we could see the big waves as they dashed against the ship. When night came, it was so dark out on the water and all we could hear was the waves dashing against the ship.

I began to meet more friends and we talked. But this one particular day, maybe the sixth or seventh day on the water, one of the soldiers said to me you get guard duty tonight. I laughed, not expecting guard duty. Sure enough, I had guard duty that night about the same time I had when I was in Georgia at the grave yard, do you remember that? This time instead of the grave yard, it was on a ship and I had to climb all the way up on a pole or little ladder that reached about one hundred feet in the air with a one, man cage that strapped me in. All I could see was the darkness of the night and the water waves that dashed against the ship, and then about two o'clock am, a light storm arose on the sea. The ship began to rock, bend and sway over. I could soon see some white form of the waves dashing in the sea. Well morning finally came and I finally got off of guard duty. What an experience! Finally, we came to the end of our destiny. We had been on the ship for ten days. We landed in London, England while it was still dark. We finally reached the England Port. We had to wait for the England Navigators to guide us through the English Channel. The fog was so thick, that I couldn't see our way through. We could only hear the sounds of horns from the other ships, as they passed by with small green and yellow lights. There was a Light House which helped to guide us through. (Later in life, I studied Jesus as being the Light House to guide His children through this dark world.) We did not get off in London, because we were going to Germany. As we arrived in Germany, men and women were there waiting and waving their hands to welcome us. We got off the ship and big army trucks were waiting for us. We got into the truck (2 ½ ton; 6 X 6; Cargo Trucks). We arrived in Erlangen, Germany.

Erlangen is a middle Franconian City in Bavaria, Germany. It is located north west of Nuremberg at the Confluence of the River Pegnitz and its large tributary, The Schwabach. We were in "C" company.

When I first arrived there, I met a young African American soldier who was there a few months before me. He told me that there was nothing downtown for us, referring to the African American soldier. Because I asked him about going downtown, later I found out the reason he said that was because downtown the Caucasian soldiers that were here before we got here (the older Caucasian soldiers), had picked and named their places to go. For the African American soldiers they named it "The Moon Shine." That made me angry, but I had to wait before I had a chance to go downtown. We had to take some shots and other things before we could even get a pass. There was one day where we got 22 shots, as we walked down the line there were doctors and nurses on both sides of us, sticking us in our arms with needles. Our arms were so sore the next day that we could hardly get out of bed.

I found out that we could not get a pass to go downtown until we finish some training. We had to go into the gas chamber. Before we went into the gas chamber room, we were taught how to fit our gas mask on so that the gas would not come in. We were told to go into the gas chamber without the gas mass on. They would ask us questions such as your name, rank and where you lived. After we would answer those questions, then we would put on the mask. It was not easy, that tear gas (It is known as Lachrymator agent or Lachrymator, which is a chemical weapon that causes severe eye, respiratory and skin irritation, pain, bleeding and even blindness.) Our eyes were hurting as we tried to answer the questions. Some of the soldiers would fall and had to be carried out. This training was harder than the training in Georgia. We were trained to have confidence in the army's protection. They would put us individually into a bunker about five hundred yards away while firing four 50 caliber machine guns. One day about mid-noon, I was placed in one of those bunkers. As the machine guns were firing, the bullets would hit the dirt and fall down into the bunker where I was. They kept firing, the bullets were hot, then while in the bunker I began to be afraid. Just as I got comfortable, a little snake about 12 inches long came out of the ground. I have always been afraid of snakes. The machine guns were still being fired and if I had climbed out of the bunker, I would have been shot so I chose to stay in the bunker with the snake. The snake crawled around the bunker which was only about a 6 X 6 bunker. It went around smelling the bullets and then crawled over my feet, as I stood perfectly still, then it went back into the hole it came out of.

Over there in Germany is what you would call "training day." This one particular day we got up early to go and train. All day long we trained until about maybe 5 pm when we stopped and the squad Sergeant lined us up and said that we had a night mission. All day we had no food and we were hungry. The Sergeant said that our food was at the end of the mission. So the Sergeant told us to go to the P.X. to buy some food. No one was supposed to know that we went to get the food, so when we got the food, we put it in our pockets to wait until we got out of their sight, but the Sergeant who told us to go and get the food, had us to line up and said, "Take everything out of our pockets," and we did. He said, "Stomp on them (our food)." We were really angry. Before he sent us out, he separated us into groups of four. Each group had one map, one poncho, one flash light and one compass. So we started out at dusk dark.

We have been out for about two or three hours now, and we still had not found the food. The woods were very dark with hilly surroundings. We began to get weary, tired, and most hungry; but we kept walking. It is now about mid-night and according to the map, we were getting close to our destiny. We came to a fence and on the other side of the fence was a stream of water, about six feet wide. On the other side of the stream was an incline that went up as though it was a mountain, it was very dark and hard to see. But we climbed over the fence and walked through the water, it was about an inch deep. When we got on top of the high slope, we could look down and see lots of lights. All of a sudden, we heard some sounds. The enemy had captured some of our men and put them in barrels and was rolling them down a steep hill; that was the sounds that we heard. The men were crying out loud. As we watched, we started to talk to one another to try to find out what was happening. Then we heard someone say, someone is over there. All four of us ran separately away. I ran the same way I came, but the others ran in different directions. I ran down the slope towards the stream of water; I could see the silhouette of the water. When I got down near the bottom of the slope, near the fence, I speedily jumped over the stream, and forgetting about the fence. I jumped and landed right into the fence, and it knocked me back into the stream of water. As I laid in the water, I looked up and saw someone standing over me. The one standing over me said to someone that was with him, where did he go? I laid in that stream of water until they left. I may have stayed there for about 15 or 20 minutes to make sure that they had left. I walked around in the woods all night; maybe an hour before day break. I was lost; I did not know where I was going until I heard some sounds. There was a soldier camp. I was not sure which camp it was. So, I waited and watched. Then one of the trucks pulled out from the camp site. I hid in the bushes until it passed by me, as the truck got a good distance from me. I ran behind the truck and made certain that no one could see me. I ran as hard as I could, but the truck went out of my sight. So, I followed the road in which the truck was headed.

As the early day was breaking, I saw a young German boy and a young German girl in the woods holding hands and talking. I was still lost, so I asked them the way out of these woods. I was glad that I could speak a little German. As I put my broken German language together, they were able to lead me out of the woods. I finally got to the main street, which is called in Germany, The Autobahn. I walked all the way back to the base. I got back to the base about mid-day, just in time to eat lunch.

Every month we got paid; all my money went to South Fallsburg Bank, in South Fallsburg, New York. I'm saying this before I found a way to make money here in the army. There were some soldiers who loved to go downtown drinking and getting with those German girls, so I would lend them money. If I loaned them $10, they would have to give me $20 back. I know that was wrong, but it was right for me. Every month on payday, I would wait outside at the mess hall (that's where the soldiers eat), for all to pay me on payday. I was making so much money that I had a Chinese man to tailor my suits. At this time, I think I finally got a chance to go downtown. Erlangen was about a ten or twenty- minute walk to the place called "The Moon Shine." All the training that we had, we didn't have time to see all of these beautiful women. I sat there drinking that German beer, and watching. I didn't know any of those women and I was downtown by myself. Just sitting there listening to the music and drinking, and watching the women. The curfew was 1 o'clock am. I had to be back at the base by 10 o'clock am, so I waited as long as I could, before walking back to the base.

We had more training. This one day we had a chemical warfare class. We sat in the classroom for hours and I began to get sleepy. The instructor was explaining what to do, if we were attacked by nerve gas. You must give yourself a shot, leaving a tag on the needle, so if you would pass out, someone would know that you had already taken the shot. As I was saying earlier, I was getting sleepy and so were others. That led the instructor to say, "The next person that goes to sleep will have to give themselves a shot with the needle." A few minutes later I heard a voice as I was trying to awake out of my sleep, but not in time, I was told to come up and stick myself with the needle. I was afraid, but also I didn't want to be a coward. I slapped my thigh hard and quickly pushed the needle in my thigh. The slapping caused my thigh to become numb.

Now we were getting into the training that we volunteered for, "Gorilla Training." That is spending a lot of time away from the base. We went out; maybe we rode about 3 or 4 hours until evening. That night after training in the woods, we laid our sleeping bags out on the ground. We were too tired to pitch tents, so we crawled into our sleeping bags and went to sleep. When morning came we had to beat our way out of the sleeping bag, because overnight it had snowed. Since we got up, we went within the camp and ate breakfast right outside. By the time I got my coffee and went to sit down, my coffee was cold and some ice had begun to form in it. It was really cold.

Well we made it through that. The next mission was very interesting. We mounted up in trucks, 2 ½ ton, which took us to a field to mount the army helicopters, which carried us to some tree line about 30 feet high, we were told to jump out and run into the woods to keep from being seen. We were fully packed, even carrying rifles. We ran into the woods at dusk dark to wait for the night to fall. At night, we were put on some small boats that was training on a maneuver attack. Maneuver is a series of moves requiring skill and care to become soldiers for real.

I had a Chinese tailor to make my suits. Going downtown, I watched the male Germans, as they sat in the Café. They sat alone with a bottle of German beer. One gentleman sat and watched from morning until mid-night; and when he left, he had a girl or a young woman with him. I found out that he was what you call a Casanova. I watched him and became a Casanova, which in America is the same as a playboy. I was dating a wonderful young girl and I found out that she had a little child, after I had given her a ring, which I had from the girl that I had back in the States. I told her that was my grandmother's ring.

This one New Year's Eve, we all met in town at a place called "Moon Shine." Maybe it was about eight or nine of us, including my date, sitting at this long table with a tall bottle of wine. It seemed to be about 2 feet high. You needed two hands to pour it out of the bottle into the glass. We drank until something the German said, "I'm tipsee!" That's the same as American's saying, I'm high! I turned and looked at my date; she was so beautiful and innocent. I looked at her and said to myself, "I can really mess her life up." She needed a man (person) in her life; and she seemed as though she wanted to be married. I was not ready for that, but now I had to try to get rid of her.

I had a really good friend while here; and he was a good man. He stayed at base a lot, and every now and then, he would go downtown. So, I couldn't leave her with just anyone. I took him over to meet her, but she didn't want him, she wanted me. I wanted her too, but I was not ready to settle down, and I had to do something. I told her to give me my ring back, but she refused. I pretended that I didn't want her anymore. It hurt me, but I had to do it. I grabbed her hand and pulled the ring off of her finger. She sort of cried, and looked sad. I got up and walked away. I felt bad about that; I really liked her, but I had to do it. A few months later,

I saw my friend and her together from a far off. They looked good together. Now, I really was happy; that was the first time I had ever gave a girl away.

When I first got over here, about two older women took me home and I spent the night with them. Also, there was a young German girl who would follow me around. I didn't know what to do with her until one day, she wanted to go to the amusement park. She wanted to ride the Ferris Wheel, and wanted me to go with her and I said, "No!" Then I thought about it and said to her, "Go on, I'll wait for you." She loved the Ferris Wheel, so when she got on and sat down, I ran away and left her, and saw her no more.

The Moon Shine was the place where all these beautiful creatures would come. There were different parts of their bodies that would seem to trap you. As I sat one summer evening in the Moon Shine watching who came in, there already in the place was a young German girl. She got up from her seat and went over to the juke box to play music. She had on a shiny white blouse, and a thin grey skirt that shaped along her body. It seemed to cast a spell on me! Next thing I knew, it was about midnight and I was walking out of the Moon Shine with her. As we walked toward the army base, I could still see in my mind, that thin grey skirt that shaped around her beautified body. As we walked toward the barracks, the highway was on the right. It was past midnight so no cars we re passing. It was quiet and the woods were on the left of the barracks. While walking with my left arm around her, my body had been close to her body rubbing against that grey skirt. I felt her thigh; not talking our bodies took control. We turned off on a path that led down into the woods.

As we stopped and stood there for a moment, there seemed to be a scene of God's creation. As she undressed piece by piece, and as she laid down on her back, I watched her milky white body in the darkness of the night. The bright moon flashed off her body, as the stars looking from above. "Maybe this is what Adam saw when Eve was created.", I said in my mind. After spending some time there, we left walking back toward the barracks, not too far away. When we got there, everyone was asleep. We climbed over the wall and went into the barracks without anyone seeing us. I took and hid her up in the attic; went to my bed, and went to sleep. When I awoke early in the morning, I went to get her, but she was gone and I never saw her again.

A few months later, I was back at the Moon Shine sitting, as I always do at a table where I could watch who was coming in, and where I could see the juke box. It was another spring but breezy night; and while I sat there, there was this young girl with long black hair and that German look. At first, I didn't see her face. She stood there selecting the song she wanted to play. Then I heard the sound of the song she had chosen to play, "Look at His Eyes, Gee Whiz", then she turned and looked at me. She caught me spell bound with her eyes, greenish staring at me like cat eyes. It seemed like I was caught in a spider's web. I found myself going to her, after she had gone back to her seat where she was sitting with a crowd of people. She sat down near a young man, maybe her date, but I couldn't help myself. I went over to her and asked the young man could I dance with her. He replied, "Ask her!" So, I did and we were dancing that dance called the "two step", because it was a slow song. I held her close to me, and I whispered in her ear that I would like a date with her, and she said, "Yes!"

The next week we met. Well, without going any further with this, let me end this story of this young black boy's experience in the woods (the world with these beautiful creatures). My time in Germany has come to an end. Now I'm back on this ship, crossing the ocean heading back to the U.S.A. While watching the ocean waters, the dark at night set upon the watch, and the waves in the early morning or late evening, my mind wondering about those beautiful creatures, who God had created. One of these days, I'm going to find one and take her home with me. The end for now!

Printed in the United States
By Bookmasters